GODALM

10
TOWN AND
COUNTRY
RAMBLES

CHRIS HOWKINS

PUBLISHED BY
CHRIS HOWKINS

PUBLISHED BY
Chris Howkins,
70 Grange Road, New Haw,
ADDLESTONE, Surrey.
KT15 3RH

PRINTED BY
Ian Allan Printing,
Coombelands House,
Coombelands Lane,
ADDLESTONE, Surrey.
KT15 1HY

TEXT AND ILLUSTRATIONS
Chris Howkins

COPYRIGHT © Chris Howkins

ISBN 0 9519348 0 5

CONTENTS

INTRODUCTION   4

LOCATION MAP OF RAMBLES   6

GODALMING TOWN CENTRE   8

GODALMING TO UNSTEAD BRIDGES   16

GODALMING TO UNSTEAD PARK   22

GODALMING TO EASHING   28

FARNCOMBE   34

JUNIPER VALLEY   40

HYDON'S BALL   44

MILFORD - WITLEY - ENTON   46

ELSTEAD   52

HANKLEY COMMON   58

LINKING THE RAMBLES   64

INTRODUCTION

GODALMING is full of surprises; it nestles beside the
River Wey among wooded hills and yet the view from the
main road gives hardly a clue to this. Godalming is a
place to abandon the car and explore on foot; out in
the woods and hills and heathlands of the district or
around town centre where even a short walk reveals a
more complete history than does any other Surrey town.
It has also the best collection of timber-framed
buildings.

THE RAMBLES have been selected to introduce some of
this variety in the landscape and its history. They are
deliberately short to leave time to look and enjoy,
rather than clock up miles. There is a page indicating
how some of the rambles can be joined together for
longer excursions. The text usually highlights possible
difficulties, such as steep hills and steps, for the
less agile.

MAPS: These are definitely only to give a visual picture
to the directions in the text; thus they are distorted
to fit the page, not drawn to scale and greatly
simplified for those who find difficulty reading maps
at all. The first map, for Town Centre, has additional
information for starting the other rambles.

RIGHTS OF WAY do not exist over the towpath of the
Godalming/Wey Navigation which belongs to the National
Trust. The public are invited to use it but the Trust
may close sections from time to time for maintenance
and undesirables may be asked to leave the property.
Similarly, the public may be excluded from some of the
other sites for conservation work etc. Basically, be
prepared to co-operate and remember that the inclusion
of any route in this book is no guarantee of a public
right of way.

BOATS: It's all very well enjoying the towpath but there is then the urge to go boating. There are two options; either hiring a boat from the Farncombe Boathouse which is where Catteshall Road crosses the Navigation, or, travelling on the horse-drawn narrowboat, from the wharf at the town end of Catteshall Lane. Both companies use the Navigation but are independant of the National Trust so waving a membership ticket does not get a reduced price. Boaters should not land on the riverbank that does not carry the towpath because it is privately owned.

THE MUSEUM for further local information is opposite the old town hall in the High Street. The **LIBRARY** is next to the town bridge in Bridge Street.

WHEELS: Guidance is given as to the suitability of the route for pushchairs and wheelchairs but it is only a guide. The dtermined will get anywhere. This information is on the map page.

The Hankley Common Ramble was produced by Mrs Jenny Roberts, who also gave assistance with Juniper Valley and Hydon's Ball routes; many thanks. My thanks also to Darren Hemsley for working on the final manuscript, assisting with Elstead, and producing the cover drawing.

Cover drawing - cottages on Brighton Road, Godalming; also reproduced on title page.

LOCATION MAP OF THE RAMBLES

RAMBLES IN THIS
NORTHERN PART OF THE
DISTRICT ARE TO BE FOUND
IN THE GUILDFORD VOLUME
IN THIS SERIES

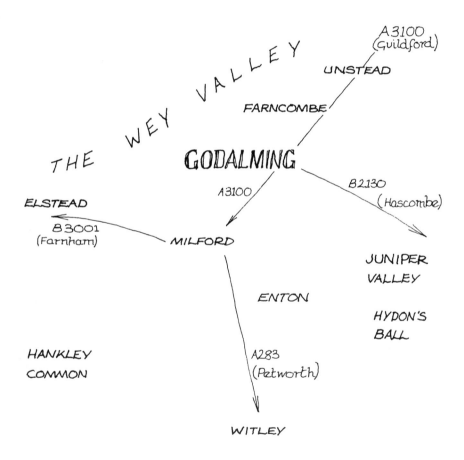

THE WEY VALLEY

A3100
(Guildford)

UNSTEAD

FARNCOMBE

GODALMING

A3100

B2130
(Hascombe)

ELSTEAD

B3001
(Farnham)

MILFORD

JUNIPER
VALLEY

ENTON

HYDON'S
BALL

HANKLEY
COMMON

A283
(Petworth)

WITLEY

Godalming church. 1982.

GODALMING: TOWN CENTRE

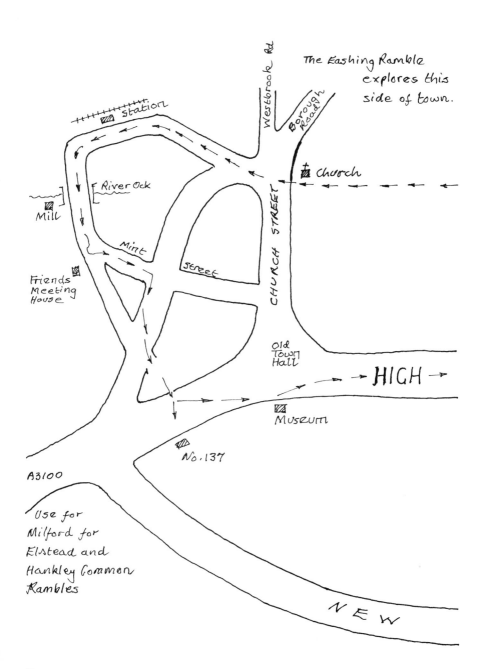

The Eashing Ramble explores this side of town.

Westbrook Rd

Borough Roadway

Station

Church

River Ock

Mill

Mint

Street

CHURCH STREET

Friends Meeting House

Old Town Hall

HIGH

Museum

No. 137

A3100

Use for Milford for Elstead and Hankley Common Rambles

NEW

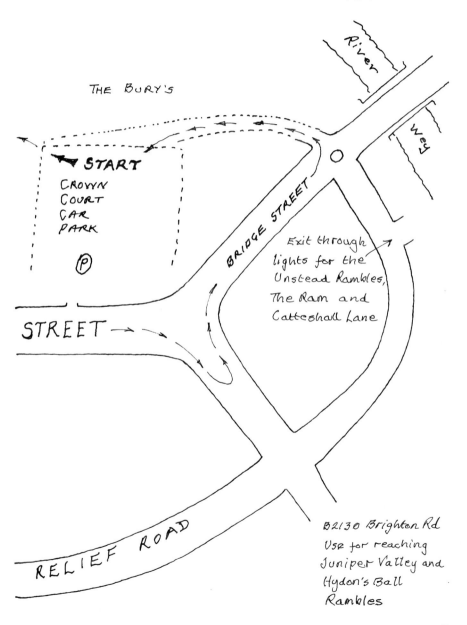

The Farncombe Ramble explores this side of the river.

River

Wey

THE BURY'S

➤ START

CROWN
COURT
CAR
PARK

Ⓟ

STREET →

BRIDGE STREET

Exit through lights for the Unstead Rambles, The Ram and Catteshall Lane

RELIEF ROAD

B2130 Brighton Rd
Use for reaching Juniper Valley and Hydon's Ball Rambles

The Burys 1981

START - CROWN COURT CAR PARK

TURN AWAY from the High Street to look downhill to the riverside, the Burys fields and Frith Hill beyond.

LEAVE by bottom left corner and bear LEFT to the end of Moss Lane and so along surfaced footway beside the wall to reach the road at Deanery Place. The wall is a fine example of the Bargate stone which has been quarried around the town for building since Romano-British times.

The route enters the churchyard from under the drooping boughs of fine mature Plane trees and affords good views of one of the finest of Surrey's few large medieval churches. The 14th century lead spire is just one of its many treasures, for which there is a good guide book available inside.

AT DEANERY PLACE look left to view Church Street with its timber-framed, Georgian and Victorian houses and then TURN RIGHT to cross the altered road junction, to walk down into the dip and up the other side to the railway station. This is Godalming's second station but even so it dates from 1859 and is therefore in a domestic style before railway fashions adopted the Gothic style.

BEAR LEFT to pass in front of the station and so down Mill Lane into an old and interesting part of the town. Hatch Mill still stands over the little River Ock and is of interest for having had its waterwheel changed to a turbine in 1940 and this can still be seen. Beyond it stands a block of the mill workers' cottages while opposite is the old Granary and Tudor Cottage. They all help to give clues as to what this narrow area was like generations ago.

Deanery
Place.

CONTINUE up the hill to Mint Street on the left.
Opposite, next to a fine timber-framed building, is the
Friends' Meeting House. It looks uninteresting from the
front but is one of the oldest in Surrey, with the
usual appealing Quaker simplicity inside, and, a small
burial ground behind, delightfully overhung with cherry

blossom in May. Godalming was an important local centre in the early days of the Quakers.

From this high level above the lane is the best place to look across to the other side to see an 18th century framework knitter's workplace built on to the back of No.22. Textiles and then framework knitting were important in Godalming – see Museum for details. Look for upper windows raised into dormers in the old houses to see where such workers lived and added more light to their workrooms.

TURN LEFT up Mint Street to the railing at the new road and look left. The second white building still has Godalming's first cinema (1911-1935) behind it; the ventilators can still be seen in the roof.

TURN RIGHT at the railing but glance left over the road to the Salvation Army Hall. This was Godalming's first Methodist Church, in 1869 after an appeal by the Minister of the Farncombe Chapel. Methodism found only a limited welcome in Godalming in its early days; John Wesley came four times but did not preach.

CROSS THE ROAD and TURN LEFT to cut up the right hand side of the Red Lion. Note the woolsack motif on the wall.

AT THE TOP there is the option of detouring to the right for a closer look at No.137 with its blue tiled front. This is a complete Art Deco shop front with none other like it in the county. The ornamental cattle heads are a reminder that this was Stovold's Dairy, 1928-1989. Coloured cattle heads survive on the Butcher's in Egham High St.

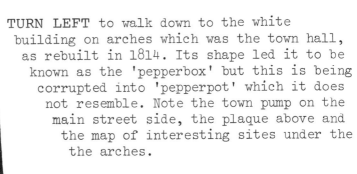

TURN LEFT to walk down to the white
building on arches which was the town hall,
as rebuilt in 1814. Its shape led it to be
known as the 'pepperbox' but this is being
corrupted into 'pepperpot' which it does
not resemble. Note the town pump on the
main street side, the plaque above and
the map of interesting sites under the
the arches.

Church Street runs off down to the
church on the left beginning with
mellow 18th century brickwork on
the right on which can still be
discerned a painted inscription:
Courage Ales Skinners Arms Ales
and Stout. There were many pubs
in Godalming, partly due to it
having its own brewery.

Another former pub is the great
timber-framed building opposite
the Pepperbox, sketched opposite.
It is unusual for Surrey in having
TWO projecting storeys. It was in
this pub, The White Hart, that
General Oglethorpe put on
exhibition, in 1734, the first
American Indians seen in this
country: 10 Yamacraws and
their chief, Tomochichi.

To the right is the town
MUSEUM, open Tuesdays to Saturdays,
from 10 till 5, admission free. Check
for special exhibitions etc. at the time
of rambling (Tel. 0483-426510)

CONTINUE ALONG THE HIGH STREET
Keep looking above the modern shop
fronts to see the older frontages.
Angel Court opens on the left
which returns ramblers to START.

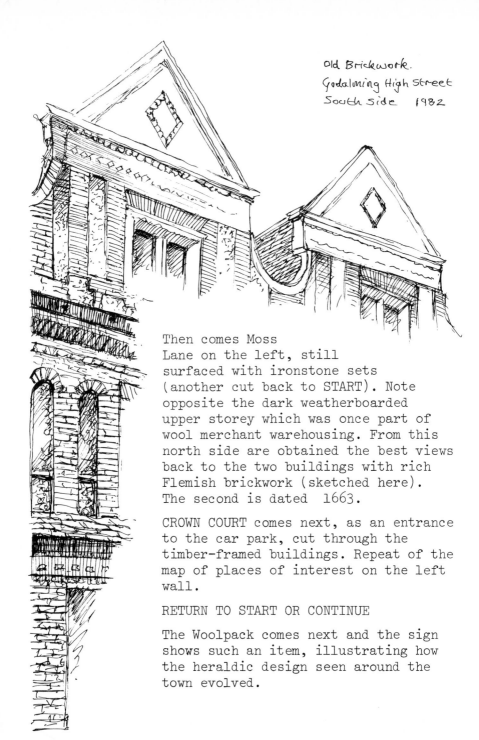

Old Brickwork.
Godalming High Street
South Side 1982

Then comes Moss
Lane on the left, still
surfaced with ironstone sets
(another cut back to START). Note
opposite the dark weatherboarded
upper storey which was once part of
wool merchant warehousing. From this
north side are obtained the best views
back to the two buildings with rich
Flemish brickwork (sketched here).
The second is dated 1663.

CROWN COURT comes next, as an entrance
to the car park, cut through the
timber-framed buildings. Repeat of the
map of places of interest on the left
wall.

RETURN TO START OR CONTINUE

The Woolpack comes next and the sign
shows such an item, illustrating how
the heraldic design seen around the
town evolved.

Opposite is Queen Street and the view up there reveals a brick building, top right, with dormer gables, which is where the Victoria car was assembled in 1907.

Next, in the High Street, is the King's Arms, refronted in 1753 and the last survivor of the town's coaching inns. Guests have included Frederick William III of Prussia and Czar Peter the Great. Opposite is The Square, with 16th century timber-framing. Note dutch gable to the right.

TURN RIGHT up Wharf Street to look between the buildings on the right to see a sensible use of mirror glass where a new building has been squeezed into a tiny space. The mirror doubles the gap and reflects the warm Bargate stone and Victorian tile-hanging opposite.

TURN BACK and RIGHT down Bridge Street. This used to be a narrow muddy way past the brewery and still keeps its Tudor timber-framed barn with adjoining cottage but first notice the impressive cut-brick frontage of 1878. Lastly comes the Borough Hall of 1906, looking all the better for trees and extensions added in recent times. Note the wool pack again, on the left bay, first granted to the Borough by Elizabeth I.

TURN LEFT to walk through The Burys back to the car park. This scene of pastureland so close to a modern town centre is a great treasure but on this side of the river it is gradually becoming suburbanised with rose beds etc. Among the nearby trees are the deciduous Swamp Cypress which remain bright pea green when in leaf, turning colour in the autumn. Although it was introduced to this country (from S.W. United States, in 1640 it is still far from commonly used.

The youth centre beside the car park commemorates local worthy, Alfred Noyce, the climber of Everest. This town has a surprisingly long list of well known people who have lived or worked here.

15

GODALMING To UNSTEAD BRIDGES
Mixed Countryside

DISTANCE : Nearly 4 miles

WHEELS : Not Suitable

PARKING : Either in a
town centre park such
as Crown Court, or,
on the roadside of
Catteshall Lane
beyond the yellow
lines.

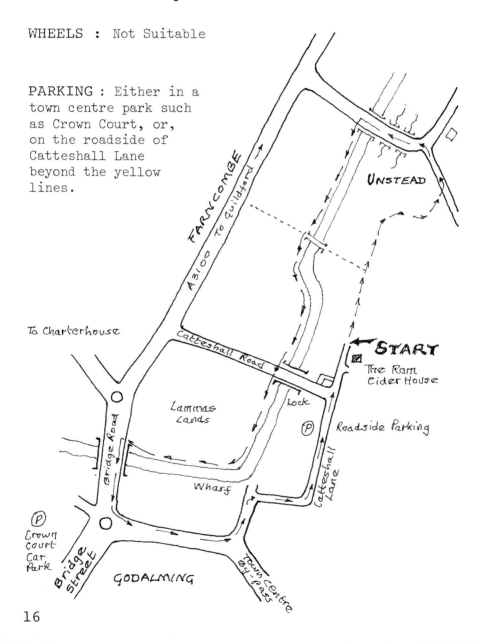

This is a rural ramble
along the wooded hill-
side and back along
the towpath through
the riverside meadows.

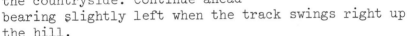

START at the Ram Cider
House in Catteshall Lane.

CONTINUE along the
level road past the pub
and so off the highway on
to a track at the edge of
the countryside. Continue ahead
bearing slightly left when the track swings right up
the hill.

Now there is more of interest. The Elms were wiped out
by Dutch Elm Disease but have now regenerated from their
roots and are now large enough to fringe the route with
thickets and break the sky overhead. In spring the
ferny leaved Hedge Parsley shoots up its stems in a
desperate effort to flower before the Elms shade out
the light.

Soon views open up on the left to surprise ramblers by
how much height has been gained already above the river
level. The meadows, green in summer, rush brown in the
winter, are backed by Frith Hill. Behind that is the
long line of the Hog's Back, dipping sharply at the far
right where the river cuts through at Guildford.

CONTINUE AHEAD AT THE CROSSROADS IN THE TRACK.
(If you turn left instead you reach the Navigation towpath and can turn left to return to Godalming.)

Come in April and be scolded by
Mistle Thrushes for invading
their nesting territory; see
the wild Arums leafing up so
brightly, including the strain
with spotted leaves

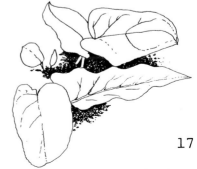

Arum
seedlings.

17

In spring also, among the vivid green shoots of the Arum, are the paler strap leaves of the Wild Garlic, thrusting up heads of white starry blooms.

The path bends to the right to climb up a coombe where a field has been scooped out of the woods, leaving the Blackthorn blossom to whiten the edges, and a Wild Cherry to overhang the top with its own white blossom. A Horse Chestnut will be budding up to continue the display. The path is bordered with massive Hazel stools from when this Ancient wood was coppiced and it is indeed one of Surrey's Ancient woods – all the indicator species are there, from Dog's Mercury, Bluebells, Wild Garlic and Wood Anemones to the tiny but beautiful Moschatel.

Wild
Garlic

TURN LEFT at the top of the field and continue up a steep gully. Such deeply sunken hidden routes through the hills carry the reputation for having guided the smugglers through the night, intent upon hiding their wares in the Juniper bushes which once grew on the heaths across the hilltop.

With the chiff-chaffs singing their arrival for the summer, and Bluebells on the right, there are views out over the Wey valley to the Hog's Back behind Peasmarsh and Loseley.

The route becomes a driveway and at the public highway **TURN LEFT**. For a short distance plunge off the hill down this sunken lane but beware of traffic on the bends.

Moschatel

18

Unstead 91

Note the old
Hazel stools in
the hedgerows again,
and, noticeable in spring,
the mauve (sometimes white)
flowers on the banks are Honesty plants – a garden
escape that naturalises well along such lanes as this.

TAKE FIRST LEFT and continue along a narrower and
even quieter lane to Unstead Bridge at the bottom, with
its decorative white railings. It is one of a series of
medieval bridges surviving along the Upper Wey. They
may date from soon after 1233 when it was recorded that
great floods damaged severely the local bridges. This
one has been somewhat altered so see notes on Eashing
bridge in another ramble for the architectural merit.

In the reign of Elizabeth I this bridge was in
"gret Ruyn and utter decay, but they do not
kno by whom it is to be repayred." Then we
find that "by the Voise of the Countrey
it is to be repayred by Sir John
Warn' and Rychard Caryll' gent."
Obviously they did a good job as
it is still here, nestling among
great clumps of Comfrey.

A very short detour to the right
offers views of Unstead Manor on
the corner – a fine timber-framed
building which has recently been
restored. For an illustrated account of
this site last century see Gertrude
Jekyll's "Old West Surrey" where it is
described as Unstead Farm.

Arum shoot

19

Unstead Manor

The riverside opposite
Unstead Manor has been
designated a site of
Special Scientific Interest
so it is important to keep
dogs and children from
invading it.

CROSS THE MEDIEVAL BRIDGE
and walk ahead to the next
bridge. FOLLOW the lane on
to a third bridge and there
TURN LEFT on to the towpath.

Follow the towpath of the Godalming
Navigation all the way to the road.
Look out for Orange Tip Butterflies which
use the Lady's Smocks in the meadows as a
food plant. On the other side of the water,
the meadows are owned by the National Trust and
are leased out to a specialist in rare breeds;
when this was being prepared he had beautiful great
Devon Red cattle there.

Soon the waters part, where surplus from the Godalming
Navigation plunges over Unstead Sluices to follow the
course of the natural river, out under Unstead Bridge
to rejoin the Navigation at Peasmarsh.

Here at Unstead Sluices the horse-drawn narrowboat turns round, during its summer season, so there is something unusual to watch but keep clear. Turning is partly by poling, in the time-honoured way.

Next of interest is Trowers Bridge, known locally as Firs Bridges, spanning the Navigation. It was built in 1789 to replace the ford that was proving dangerous once the river had been deepened to make it navigable. When the central span was made of planks they could be removed to allow high loads through, such as bark for the tanneries. Note attractive timber-framed cottage on the right.

CROSS ROAD at Farncombe Boathouse (boats for hire) to continue along towpath (right side of Catteshall Lock). On the bend opposite the Wharf there is a post bearing a vertical roller; it's for guiding towropes round the corner. Although it looks old it was made and installed by the National Trust in 1989.

TURN LEFT at the road (Bridge Road) and cross the bridge to return to town centre.

Mallard drake

GODALMING ᴛᴏ UNSTEAD PARK
Wooded Hills and Riverside

DISTANCE : *4 miles approx.*
Can be lengthened or shortened.

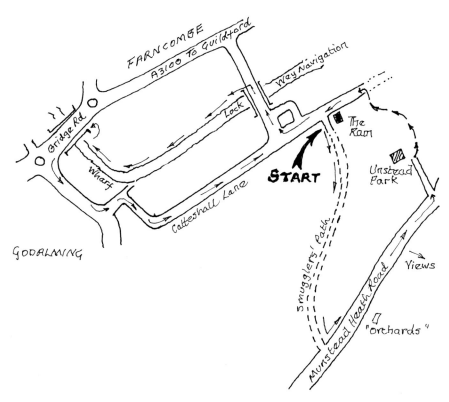

WHEELS : Not suitable.

PARKING : Roadside parking in Catteshall Lane. As this
is a long road with the minimum of interest, try to
find a space as soon as the yellow lines end in order
to share it out between the start and the end of the
ramble. Users of town centre car parks can pick up the
route at the end of Catteshall Lane (ask for Sainsbury's).

Up the hill, along the top, down again – very simple and easy to follow and always rewarding, whether the hollows be full of spring flowers or the golden leaves of autumn.

START at the Ram Cider House at the end of Catteshall Lane.

TURN UP THE HILL IN FRONT OF THE PUB and **CONTINUE AHEAD** when the road becomes a track.

Note the entrance to Catteshall Manor on the right. It was Henry I who is thought to have separated this manor off from Godalming and passed it to the Purcell family for services rendered. Geoffrey Purcell was the usher in charge of the linen and the laundresses, before it all got too much for him and he retreated to Reading Abbey to be a monk. He gave these lands to the Abbey. Later holders included Thomas Holland, Earl of Kent, (1383) and William More (1565) of nearby Loseley.

Next of note...

...is the impressive long timber-framed farmhouse shown on the previous page. It stands up on the slope on the left of the route and does not just LOOK long but IS long, for having an extra bay in its construction compared with the norm in Surrey. There are other rather individual features about it too which have led to the suggestion that this house was involved in some way with the local textile industry when it was first built.

After this the lane cuts steadily and attractively through trees up the hillside; not TOO steeply but giving nevertheless the impression of climbing into the hills.

Go quietly; you never know what you might see. Even on a Good Friday lunch time we startled out a Roe Deer and the local gardeners will assure you that there are plenty of those around here. Then there was the chance to watch a fox watching rabbits – scores of rabbits in the field dipping down to the right of the route. There was a rich variety of bird life too.

TURN LEFT at the top when the road is reached.

Follow this attractive lane through the trees, perhaps trying to imagine it as a sandy surface from the days when it was well known to Gertrude Jekyll who lived nearby. Her great associate, the architect Sir Edwin Lutyens knew it too. Here, on the right, he built one of his particularly famous houses – "Orchards" in 1899. Even the glimpse we get from the road is impressive. (Sketch opposite).

CONTINUE along the lane, which follows the crest of the hill and affords wonderful wide views eastwards as soon as the trees thin out. As the lane begins to climb ....

Part of orchards
1991

TURN LEFT up the driveway to Unstead Park and nearer the main entrance follow the signposted public path off to the **RIGHT** and KEEP to this path from now onwards, ignoring tempting sidepaths. At first the route passes through trees and then opens out through the parkland. There are views back to Unstead Park house, built c.1780 and considered one of the best of the lesser houses of that date in Surrey.

Head downhill all the way and soon the route swings to the left and joins the highway that returns ramblers to the Ram pub – named after the hydraulic water ram in the bank opposite. It raises water to places up the hill and was installed in the 1920s. Continue to the junction with Catteshall Road and...

TURN RIGHT to follow Catteshall Road down to the river. The remains of Catteshall Mill stand on the right; not very old although the milling site is one

25

listed in the Doomsday Book (1086). Corn, wool, leather and paper have all been processed here.

CROSS THE BRIDGE On the right is Farncombe Boathouse (c.1908) from where boats can be hired, while from the left railing of the bridge the working of Catteshall Lock can be watched without getting in the way.

TURN LEFT off the far end of the bridge and through the gate to follow the towpath upstream. This first straight stretch is the Godalming Navigation, opened in 1764, and soon the junction is reached where the old course of the river is still followed by excess water, running off to the mill. In this wide pool the barges used to be turned round and pulled in reverse up to the wharf when that was too congested for them to be turned there. They were turned by poling, as can still be seen at the wharf when the horse-drawn narrow-boat has to be turned for its outward journey.

Bullfinch

Looking across at the wharf, note the black weather-boarded building which is thought to date back to when the wharf first opened. It is still used in part as a stable. This is the southernmost point of the British Inland Waterways system.

TURN LEFT on reaching the road. On the right is the Godalming United Church, built in 1903 although the town has been a centre of Non-conformity since the early days and in the case of Methodism can be traced back to the visits of John Wesley himself.

AHEAD is the town centre. The turning right off the roundabout returns ramblers to the central car park. The turning left leads to Catteshall Lane and the starting point of this ramble.

Giant Balsam, Impatiens glandulifera
syn. Impatiens roylei, introduced 1839
and now wild along the river bank.

GODALMING to EASHING

DISTANCE : 4 miles approx

WHEELS: not suitable.

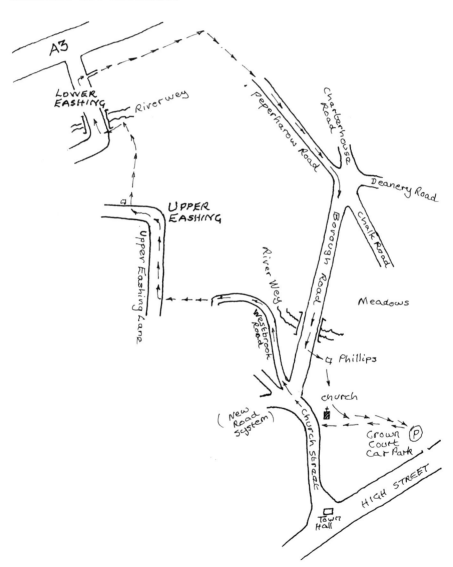

This ramble goes
out from town, up
over the hill to
drop down to the
Wey at Eashing
and back along the
river valley to
the Farncombe end
of the town. Apart
from the early hill
it is easy walking
through a variety
of town and country.

START at the central car park and leave by the lower
left corner to turn left and follow the route through
to the Church and Deanery Place.

TURN RIGHT at Deanery Place, **CROSS** Borough Road and
TURN RIGHT into Westbrook Road and follow this leafy
lane right to the top of the hill.

Note on the left the great Georgian mansion, Westbrook
House (now the Meath Home) where lived General James
Oglethorpe (Lived 1696-1785), local M.P. and founder
of the State of Georgia. The next owner was Nathaniel
Godbold (monument in church) who had recently made his
money as an early developer of patent medicines.

Near the hilltop, on the right is a newer Westbrook,
built as the home of the local architect of note, Hugh
Thackeray Turner (memorial in church) who was working
with local materials in a style influenced by Voysey.
This had a Gertrude Jekyll garden but now only some of
her tree plantings survive.

At the top, where the road turns sharp left, **CONTINUE AHEAD, through the gate** and follow the gravelled driveway to the end and out by another gate. The Victorian cottages (right) on the right were not built as such but have evolved out of farm buildings from when this was all part of the great Westbrook Estates.

Through the gate and CONTINUE AHEAD, along the bridleway over what is suddenly a wide broad hilltop of farmland. Look out for flocks of Linnets etc. feeding on weed seeds. The farm buildings en route are not very attractive but wait till the next set is reached.

TURN RIGHT at the road. Next come the farmsteads worth waiting for. This attractive settlement is Upper Eashing which is one of the surprises that Surrey is so good at providing. Follow the lane round to the left and look for a public footpath sign on the right just before Dean Cottage.

TURN RIGHT over stile and head straight across the top of the field, along its shoulder above the steep valley on the right. Ignore the paths worn by the sheep; they do not keep to the footpath. The church spire on the horizon is Shackleford's.

CROSS STILE IN HEDGE left of power cable support. Take the steps that lead down through the steep woods to the river, which can be glimpsed through the trees almost under your feet. Then the route runs along the waterside to Lower Eashing, another very attractive spot, with one of the set of medieval Wey bridges (cf Unstead).

TURN RIGHT AND CROSS BRIDGE

Before crossing the bridge there is the option of a
short detour ahead to view the old cottages (below)
restored in memory of Hugh Thackeray Turner, who,
apart from being an architect, was also instrumental
in preserving parts of Surrey including these cottages
which he gave to the National Trust in 1922. Beyond is
the mill of which there has been one here since before
Doomsday (1086). In the 1630s it became Surrey's 2nd
paper mill and later it was here that paper was made
in rolls as opposed to sheets. That was under the ownership of Pewtress, Lowe and Pewtress who built the row
of workers' cottages (hence 'Pewtress Cottages') when
they had to rebuild the mill after a great fire in 1852.

The set of bridges, of which this is one, has the unique
characteristic of semi-circular cutwaters instead of
the standard triangular ones. Why the norm was changed
has never been explained.

Eashing.

31

AFTER CROSSING THE BRIDGE CONTINUE UP THE LANE THAT BECOMES THE LITTLE STREET OF EASHING. It is always attractive here but especially so with the pots of summer flowers. There are views back to the hills just crossed, where the first Normans dug themselves in. Look out for the Old Forge on the left for opposite is a farm drive down between two timber-framed houses....

TURN RIGHT

Stay on this farm road as it cuts down the valley through horse pastures and woodlands.

Watch out for the Kestrels which have their territory here and can be seen hunting over the fields. Less easy to miss are the noisy Mallard down on the river.

The wet areas are a colourful display in summer of Irises, Meadowsweet, Hemp Agrimony, Yellow and Purple Loosestrife; plus the less common like the Hesperis illustrated. Up on the drier banks grow teasels, which were still a commercial crop last century. They had been introduced hundreds of years before to serve the local textile industry – their spiky seed heads were used to fluff up woolen cloth. High class knitwear is still fulled in this way today.

The farm road ends but the route continues as a path through the woods. Keep to this and at the crossroads of paths at the end, **TURN RIGHT.**

32

FOLLOW the driveway to the
end and take the footpath
that leads off from the
left side of a gateway.
This narrow path leads
through the riverside
woods to the end of
Peperharow Road. It is
said to be part of an
ancient route that
led through to the
Saxon settlement of
Peper Harow, a little
further up the valley
from Eashing.

CONTINUE to the
end of Peperharow Rd.
where there is a choice.

Bush
vetch.

EITHER CROSS the junction
to continue ahead down Chalk Road,
OR
TURN RIGHT and follow Borough Road.

The first option brings you to the end of
Bridge Road to turn right and cross the
river to return to town centre.

The second option is more interesting. After
crossing the river TURN LEFT into the Phillips
Memorial Cloister, built in 1913 "to the heroic
wireless operator who went down with the Titanic."
It is the work of Hugh Thackeray Turner and had
a Gertrude Jekyll planting scheme.

From here there are views up to the Norman
tower of the parish church, which has
Saxon work inside. Therefore skirt
round to the left to reach the central
car park which can be seen from here.
It is also possible to go to the right
of the church and then left round
behind it.

Creeping cinquefoil (enlarged)

FARNCOMBE: Riverside and Streets

DISTANCE: 3½ miles approx.

WHEELS: keep to the surfaced areas.

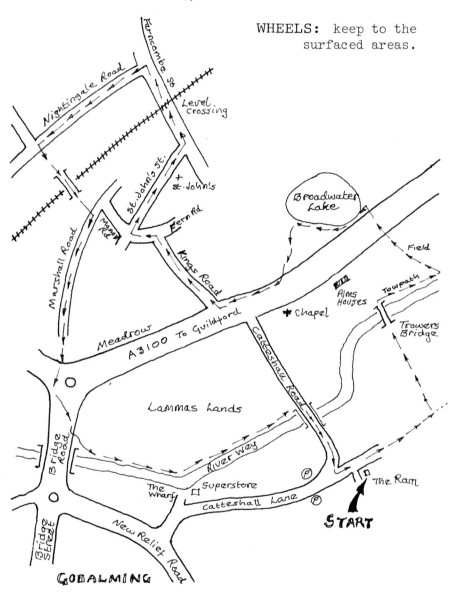

START at The Ram pub in Catteshall Lane and proceed past it till the road ends and then follow the track on keeping left to avoid the right fork.

FOLLOW the footpath along the hillside through the trees and when a little crossroads is reached **TURN LEFT.**

FOLLOW path down to the Navigation and after crossing Trowers Bridge **TURN RIGHT** along the towpath in front of this attractive cottage (sketched right).

FOLLOW towpath through a small gate and look out for a stile in the left hand fence.

TURN LEFT OVER STILE and cross field by keeping diagonally left and to the right of the oak tree. You can see over on the right a 1940s pillbox: one of some 5,000 built as a defence line from Bristol to Chatham. This is the only National Trust one.

The footpath over the field approaches the busy main road so keep children and dogs under control.

CROSS the B3100 to Broadwater Lake beyond; a good place for wildlife at quiet times, such as Great Crested Grebes and Canada Geese.

FOLLOW the shore anticlockwise until it bears more sharply to the right and there turn off **LEFT** through the trees up to the recreation ground and skirt **LEFT** round the golf course to the club house and the car park to rejoin the road. The scrub on the left of this section is rich in wildlife - butterflies, wild flowers and warblers, in early summer.

TURN RIGHT to follow the main road for a short way, to see some of Farncombe's better architecture: the front of the cottage sketched overleaf, the almshouses, the Unitarian Chapel and Meadrow House.

Wyatt's Almshouses were completed in 1622 in accordance with the will of local landowner, Richard Wyatt of the Carpenter's Company. Places were to be allocated to the elderly from the local parishes where he held land, (five places for Godalming). The matching ranges round the main block were added in 1957-8.

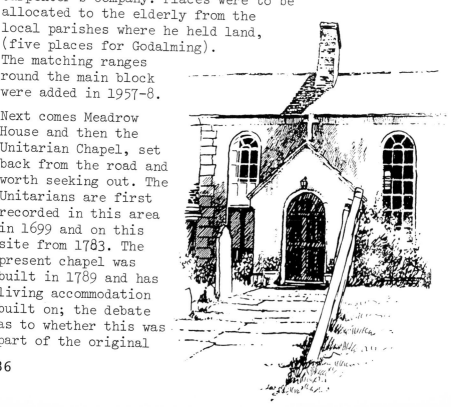

Next comes Meadrow House and then the Unitarian Chapel, set back from the road and worth seeking out. The Unitarians are first recorded in this area in 1699 and on this site from 1783. The present chapel was built in 1789 and has living accommodation built on; the debate as to whether this was part of the original

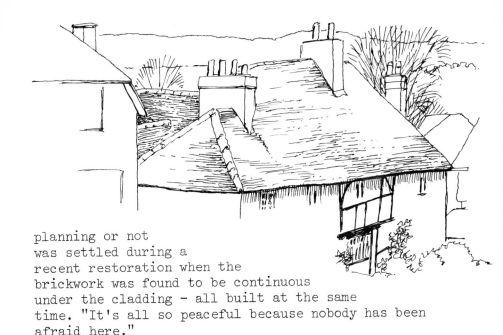

planning or not
was settled during a
recent restoration when the
brickwork was found to be continuous
under the cladding - all built at the same
time. "It's all so peaceful because nobody has been
afraid here."

TAKE FIRST RIGHT (Kings Road) to explore Farncombe.
At first it seems all post-railway (with some very good
examples of workers' terraces) but there are surprises
like the timber-framed house above remaining from the
pre-railway days.

LEFT AT END (Fern Road)

RIGHT AT END (St.John's Street). There are reminders
along here of the development of the community, such
as the Baptist Centre on the right and, on the left,
the Farncombe Progressive Club which the less progressive
found far too socialist and started calling it "Moscow".
Then comes the church of St.John the Evangelist from
when this became a separate parish from Godalming in
1849. The church was built in stages, in 1847, 1860
and 1875, by Sir George Gilbert Scott, or more likely
by his firm, as this is not a masterpiece. Nevertheless
it is built of local stone rather than Victorian red
brick so it has a pleasing texture and rich warm colour.

**BEAR LEFT, GO OVER THE LEVEL CROSSING AND
CONTINUE AHEAD** to find older parts of Farncombe.

This street is older than the 19th century expansion – note the cottage on the corner of Tottenham Road with its Bargate stone, galleted mortar and tile hanging of handmade tiles.

Opposite is a plain Georgian frontage to an older cottage (Fircot) and another Bargate cottage was given ashlar facing at the corner of Nightingale Road (down which this route proceeds, but first explore on up a bit). On the right is the timber-framed house with later ends illustrated on previous page and on the left another timber-framed block (detail below), while up on the right hand bend there is Tudor Cottage. Now turn back to Nightingale Road.

PROCEED ALONG NIGHTINGALE ROAD which was one of the first roads to be created as Farncombe developed. Here were the manorial fields, with more arable than pasture, until the railway cut through two of them in 1849. The road was built by 1851 but had no houses; ten years later there were nine.

PAUSE at the little crossroads outside The Cricketers. This was one of the first new buildings. In 1861 the publican was Harvey Trevalt who was also a plumber and painter; publicans normally doubled up as something else in those days. His sons were a shoeing smith, a millwright, and still being educated.

By turning right at this point and climbing to the top of the hill wide views over the valley can be enjoyed but, be warned, it is very steep. Instead..

TURN LEFT and proceed down to the footbridge over the railway. Looking over the right parapet is to look

onto the site of the first local railway station. It was built in 1849 and named 'Godalming' but by 1859 the present Godalming station was needed and built, nearer to the town. In 1897 the present Farncombe Station was opened leaving this first one to serve for goods only. It is still possible, despite modern development, to see where the sidings came off the main track. One of the last and most important freights was the paper from Catteshall Mill.

TURN RIGHT off the bridge and follow Marshall Road all the way into the cul-de-sac from where it continues as a not unattractive footway down the hill to the meadows at the end of Bridge Street.

CROSS the junction and continue up Bridge Street to the bridge. First, on the left, comes a tall hard red brick building with an inscription high up revealing that it was built as Godalming's Technical Institute by Surrey County Council. Before such Authorities came into being the church and the people had to provide for local needs. This is illustrated by the next main building, the British School, founded in 1812. The corner stone was laid by local landowner, Chauncey Hare Townsend of Busbridge Hall in 1813. By 1872 it needed extending and this time the lord of the manor came to set the memorial stone. Such ventures fuel dissention between the Anglican Establishment and Non-conformists and this was no exception. The vicar, for example, refused to attend the ceremony.

CONTINUE AHEAD FOR TOWN CENTRE.
Turn left at the first roundabout to reach the end of Catteshall Lane and the starting point of this ramble.

Turn right to reach the central car park,

OR

return via towpath
as shown on the map.

JUNIPER VALLEY : Hilly Woodland Ramble

DISTANCE : 4 miles approx.

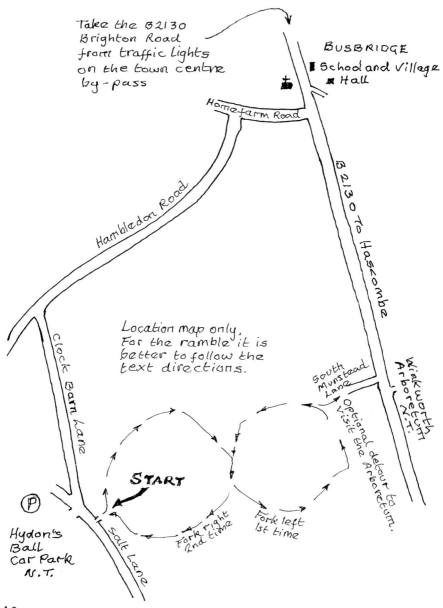

Take the B2130
Brighton Road
from traffic lights
on the town centre
by-pass

BUSBRIDGE
School and Village
Hall

Home Farm Road

Hambledon Road

B2130 To Hascombe

Clock Barn Lane

Location map only.
For the ramble it is
better to follow the
text directions.

South Munstead Lane

Winkworth Arboretum N.T.

Optional detour to visit the Arboretum.

START

P

Hydon's Ball Car Park N.T.

Salt Lane

Fork right 2nd time

Fork left 1st time

40

Along shady woodland paths and grassy rides, through open plantations and around the edges of little fields, this ramble is quietly beautiful and peaceful. It is ideal for a winter outing, being free from deep mud and with plenty of trees to break the wind.

BEWARE: there are little paths all over the place. The directions here refer to main paths only (very often those wide enough to take a vehicle).

PARKING : Hydon Ball Car Park or the Salt Lane roadside.

START : On Salt Lane, opposite entrance to Hydon Ball car park, (grid reference SU 979403). Take the signed footpath under the oak tree, that leads through a few trees on to a woodland ride.

TURN LEFT on to the woodland ride and PAUSE and TAKE NOTE of where you are as you will need to recognise this spot to return to the car. Proceed ahead.

TAKE LEFT FORK and the trees change to the Sweet Chestnut that produces the edible fruits (right) familiar about Christmas time. Notice the trees are multi-stemmed from a single base; these are old coppice stools from when chestnut plantations were of economic importance in S.W.Surrey. Some chestnut is still used for fencing.

TURN RIGHT AT THE T-JUNCTION AND PROCEED AHEAD ignoring the option of turning right again and then ignore a left option. The main track now begins to peter out but continue ahead through the trees and down the hillside. In spring there are still bluebells, primroses and wood sorrel blooming here, indicating that this was once ancient oak woods; some of the old broad-leaved trees still survive.

Puff-balls

TURN RIGHT on to the track that follows the valley bottom.

Anyone with children
running ahead should know
there is a deep gully
coming up and that it
can be full of deep water.

Larch cones

CONTINUE AHEAD at the
crossroads of tracks and
the gully pond is then
immediately on the right,
partly hidden by the
fringe of undergrowth.

The track now reaches the centre of the figure-of-eight
route chosen for this ramble. **FORK LEFT** on to the
track with the blue waymarking. Follow this over the
brow of the hill and alongside a little field which is
obviously of great age - see the massive Hazel stools
on the boundary bank. How many generations have they
been there? Gasp on up the steep hill! Next, the route
levels off to cross the crest of the hilltop and just
when it begins to drop down slightly (about halfway
along as you view it) look left for a grassy ride that
runs off at right angles.

TURN LEFT to follow this ride (the actual turning is a
bit obscured by undergrowth that sprang up when a fallen
tree blocked the way). This is a pleasant grassy ride
through the Larch trees - bright green in spring and
yellow in autumn. Towards the end of the
year look for seed-eating birds among
the cones.

Look for Goldcrests in the conifers.

42

BEAR RIGHT at the end of this grassy ride through the Larches and continue ahead, down the hill, to the gate at the bottom.

TURN LEFT beyond the gate.
(By turning right instead, the track can be followed up to the highway where it emerges opposite the entrance to Winkworth Arboretum; National Trust.)

Having turned left, follow the track across the hillside. There is quite a variety of wild flowers in their season because there are so many breaks in the tree canopy to let the sun through. Soon the route cuts across a hillside with a track coming up the valley bottom from the right. This will join the crossing point of the figure-of-eight route. This time be sure to **BEAR RIGHT** at the fork and follow YELLOW markers.

Now the dominant tree changes from the evergreen conifers to deciduous Larch, the Japanese Larch, introduced in 1861. Their reddish orange twigs in winter distinguish them from the yellow twigged European Larch. The cone scales of the former are turned over at the edges.

Cross-leaved Heath, Whortle and Gorse still survive from the days when this was open heathland. The Junipers that gave the place its name seem to be extinct.

This route begins to circle round in a clockwise direction and it is time to start looking out for; the point of entry in order to return to the road and the start.

It will be a turning left.

Wood Melick

greater
Stitchwort

43

HYDON'S BALL : Wooded Hill

DISTANCE : Wander at Will

MAP to locate this site is provided at the start of the Juniper Valley ramble.

WHEELS : Not suitable

LOCATION: 3 miles south of Godalming.
From the Godalming Relief Road (Flambard Way) take the B2130 (Brighton Road) towards Hascombe. TURN RIGHT at the top of the hill (Busbridge) into Home Farm Road and then LEFT immediately along Hambledon Road. Take FIRST LEFT into Clockbarn Lane and at the first road junction the entrance to the car park is opposite (look for the grey National Trust sign).

HYDON'S BALL is a pleasant piece of wooded country-side, rising to 593 feet. It featured regularly in the old guide books for being one of Surrey's famous view-points. Ramblers will find that it is only a short climb to the top and that the route is easy to follow. It has, therefore, been selected as the "Wander At Will" spot in this book for those who dislike following directions all the time.

TO REACH THE SUMMIT FOLLOW the track from the bottom car park up through the woods to the crest. There, TURN OFF RIGHT and climb uphill through the trees. On a hot day the walk through the mature open woodland is shady and pleasant with the shafts of light coming through. It is not an especially steep climb.

FOR A LONGER APPROACH, do not turn off at the crest but continue over the top and down the other side until there is a main turning right. Here there is a National Trust ownership signboard. TURN RIGHT, heading for the barrier to stop unwanted vehicles. Just follow this track up and round to the right and it will arrive at the summit.

At the summit is the memorial seat to Octavia Hill
(1838-1912) in whose memory this site was purchased.
She was co-founder of the National Trust and a great
enthusiast of such rural scenes as this. Sadly the
famous view from this hill-top is becoming increasingly
obscured by scrub woodland. It all used to be open
heathland as indicated by the remaining whortleberry
bushes struggling to survive in the shade of the new
trees.

Even though the panorama has gone there is still a
good look out over the Surrey and Sussex Weald to the
South Downs beyond. There are also views of the Blackdown range of hills, closing off the western Weald to
the right. On this side of the Blackdown hill lived
Sir Robert Hunter, another co-founder of the National
Trust.

Look out for an unusual plant here; the evergreen
creeping shrub making low thickets over the hilltop.
It has spikes of pale pinkish white bell-shaped
flowers followed by berries and is Gaultheria Shallon.
It was introduced to this country in 1846 from
western North America. In Britain it was used on some
estates as game cover and has now established itself
in the wild on several sandy Surrey sites, such as
here and on Leith Hill. The genus is named after an
18th century Doctor Gaultier, physician and botanist
in Quebec.

Gaultheria
Shallon

MILFORD ~ WITLEY ~ ENTON

DISTANCE : 4 miles approx.

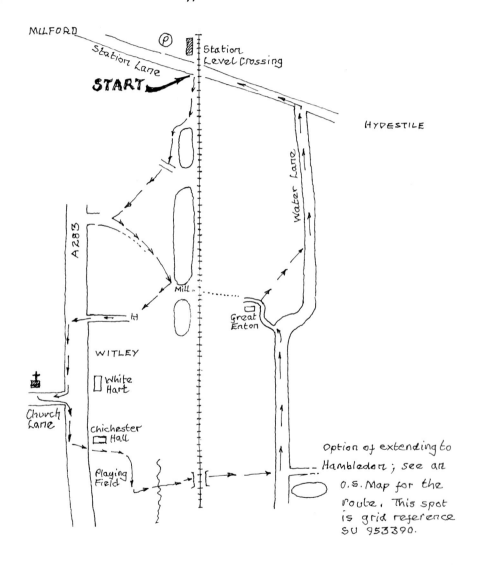

WHEELS ; Not suitable (stepping stones over stream etc).

Lakes and streams, woods and fields, mill complex and
Saxon church - this ramble has a bit of everything and
is suitable for anyone nervous of getting lost in the
countryside as this route is clear to follow.

Maywead 2.7.91

START

Milford Station.
Take footpath south
beside the line. It
begins on the Milford
edge of the level
crossing.

The footpath passes through the
woods where bird life can be good
due to the evergreens for winter shelter.
Furthermore, the woodland floor is wet with a small
stream running through it, so it remains unfrozen for
a longer time in the winter, due to the partial shelter
of the overhead trees - a good place for woodcock, if
you are very lucky and sharp-eyed.

Enton Lakes (private trout fisheries) are on the left.
There is not public access here but there are breaks in
the screening through which the Geese, Great Crested
Grebes, etc. can be observed.

This route becomes a trackway and reaches the main drive
to the fisheries. **CROSS** this drive to continue ahead
along more of the footpath (look for 'no cycling' sign).
Note, from the driveway, the Weeping Beech down on the
left - one of the more significant trees in Surrey.

TURN LEFT at the end, by Witley Men's Club, and follow
the track down to Enton Mill. It's a pretty little lane,
just as they all were a hundred years ago. There are
glimpses of some of the other Enton lakes too.

Nuthatch.

Great
Crested
Grebe
posturing

The waterside complex of Enton Mill is very attractive. As a corn milling site it is said to date back to the 15th century but operations ceased in 1899. That was just at the right time, in architectural terms, for the building of what we see today, in local style and with local materials, in what has since become known as 'The Surrey Style'.

Just as the track swings left on to the causeway, look for a gate into the field on the right. It has a yellow way marker.
   TURN RIGHT through the gate and take the clear path diagonally up across the field. Don't forget to look back for views of the mill (beautiful with Wisteria in late May).

CROSS STILE AND BEAR RIGHT to follow the next narrow trackway, with good views off to the north. BEWARE, this track leads straight out on to the A283 so children and dogs need a watchful eye. The cottages herald the approach to the road and to the historic old village of Witley.

CROSS THE A283 AND TURN LEFT to follow the road to the church. It's not far so ignore the traffic; indeed there are some attractive old cottages and an example of Surrey black weatherboarding to distract attention from the traffic.

TURN RIGHT into Church Lane and there on the right are the old cottages and church steps that seem to be illustrated in every book on Surrey. It is picturesque though isn't it? Proceed to the church, known to many well known 19th century figures like Birket Foster and George Eliot who brought their friends to explore this area. Glance up at the south wall of the church and there is the narrow window from the Saxon building. Look at the west end to see the stones set in their ancient herringbone pattern.

Woodcock

49

Step inside, to see the most complete set of wall paintings in Surrey.

Other interest includes the medieval screen and the brass to Thomas Jones (left) who was Sewer of the Chamber (i.e. food taster) to Henry VIII. The church and manor have had many royal connections, for Witley was always an important place, being on the main route to Shoreham on the coast for shipping across to France when the English still held French lands.

RETURN TO THE A283
The White Hart opposite is attractive and one of the sites with royal associations - was this where Edward I held Court in 1305? The white hart was one of the badges of Richard II; he gave Witley to his nurse who was married to his tailor.

TURN RIGHT and walk the short distance to Chichester Hall and **CROSS OVER** to enter the Recreation Field next to it. Begin to circle the field clockwise and **LEAVE** by the first exit down in the far corner.

FOLLOW the path into the woods and **BEAR LEFT** to cross the stream by the causeway and the wooden stepping posts. Proceed ahead through the woodland to go through the narrow railway arch.

Proceed ahead through more beautiful woodland - birch, pine and bracken - to the road. Opposite is another lake, complete with swans. From this point (grid ref. SU 953391) there are options for continuing eastwards (see OS map 186) to the pretty village of Hambledon.

TURN LEFT out of the
woodland and follow
the highway - a quiet
country lane with views
back across the valley
to Witley. Early on,
the great fir trees with
reddish brown trunks are
Douglas Firs, introduced
from North America in 1827
and named after the explorer
and collector David Douglas.
The evergreen ferns on the
bank further on belong to the
Polypody group. They were used
formerly as a mild laxative
and in cough medicines.

AT THE FIRST JUNCTION , at the
bottom of a hill, where the main
highway swings right, take the
bridleway track off to the left, to the
farm and cottages of Great Enton. Where the
track swings left round the corner of a farm
building there is a choice: either, to continue
ahead on the track, or, turn right and take the signed
footpath off across the field.

IF you continue on the track it will lead back to Enton
Mill from where the route can be retraced back to the
start.

IF you take the footpath it leads back to the highway
where you turn LEFT and then LEFT AGAIN to the station.
This option is slightly shorter and more level than to
return via Enton Mill. It is the route shown on the
sketch map.

ELSTEAD : Village and Heathland

DISTANCE : 3 miles approx.

WHEELS: Possible in village section
but not on heath.

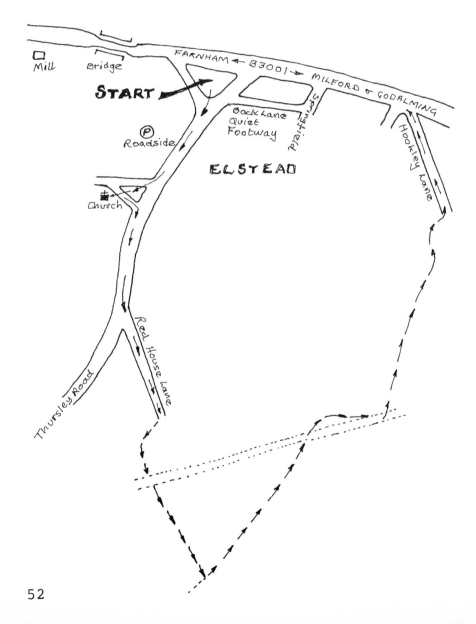

LOCATION : Elstead lies some four miles from the town centre of Godalming, via Milford, on the B3001 road to Farnham.

ON THE WAY look out for views of Oxenford on the right of the B3001 after Milford. The folly ruin, gatehouse and great barn seen reflected in the foreground water are a prime example of the Victorian sense of the picturesque, and the finest Gothic Revival work by Pugin the architect.

Oxenford 4/93

Woolpack
Skyline

ELSTEAD is only a small village but rewarding all the same because it can be deceptive; it is so easy to miss some of the very old cottages because they hide their age behind modern additions. What looks new from one angle suddenly becomes 16th or 17th century from another angle. Several show they were built originally as 'open hall' houses. In earlier times Elstead was one of many local villages that was involved in the local wool trade, hence pub names like the Wool Pack and the Golden Fleece.

PARKING on the roadside, such as Thursley Road.

START on the little village green beside the B3001. This ramble goes away from the road but before doing that there is the option of visiting the old bridge and the mill, which is now a restaurant. Unfortunately they are just ahead on the B3001 where motorists hurtle into the narrowness of the bridge. Take care.

The bridge is thought by some to belong to the same set as Eashing and Unstead but has had a lot of patching. The mill is an 18th century brick and tile building that gets described as the best in the county by the architecture experts. There has been a mill here since early medieval times, working corn and malt and fulling for the cloth industry.Its last work was making worsted braid and that had ceased by 1878.

FROM THE VILLAGE GREEN walk away from the B3001, along Thursley Road to the church. Note the great Cedar tree in the churchyard which is quite a rarity for not having had its lower branches removed. Thus we can see it in its full majesty sweeping its boughs down into the headstones. It was planted in 1849 as a thanksgiving by those who escaped an outbreak of cholera. Next, look up at the oak-shingled spire and notice the white weather boarded tower which is a rarity in Surrey; normally such would be shingled like the spire. Now move round to the north door and note the timber doorframe which is a national rarity. Notice the two pieces of timber have been split from the same log. Inside there is a good Surrey example of timber tower supports and, if the door is unlocked, there is a medieval ladder up to the bells; it has the treads cut from a solid tree trunk. There are other items of interest, despite the medieval church being rather Victorianised last century.

CONTINUE UP THURSLEY RD. TURN LEFT after the school into Red House Road. Along here the gardens are well established and have a particularly rewarding collection of plants. Spring leaves, blossom and bulbs colour a visit in Spring and there are fine autumn tints at the other end of the season. This whole district has had some notable nurseries in the past and at Elstead was that of Ernest Ladham who introduced many new cultivars, often bearing the Elstead name, notably Hypericum inodorum 'Elstead' which received an Award of Merit in 1933.

Cheiranthus species.

BEAR RIGHT at the end of the
lane before the gate to the
farm, onto a track into the
heathland. Keep ahead; do not
bear off any further to the
right. There can be puddles
in the ruts to start with but
there are ways round these.

STRAIGHT ON at the crosstracks.
There is a much greater sense of open space
by now and typical Surrey heathland scenery with its
own range of birds, butterflies and moths etc. to look
out for.

TURN LEFT AT THE T-JUNCTION. The heathland on the
right is the edge of the famous Thursley Heath Nature
Reserve, our finest lowland acid bog, with many rare
and weird species of wildlife, but, do not go plunging
off through there as it can be deep and dangerous in
places. The stands of mature pines along this route
are Scots Pines, Pinus sylvestris, which may look very
grand here but which can become a terrible weed among
the heather where the heathland needs conserving.

BEAR RIGHT at the next crosstracks onto the wider
track and look out for a route off to the left. FORK
LEFT onto this bridleway and follow it through woods
once more. Note the change in the habitat, with more
bracken and broad-leaved trees, such as oak. The wildlife will change accordingly. KEEP LEFT when the
field comes into view between the trees. Now there is
a richer variety in the trees and the ground flora. In
the spring there are the bright bluish
purple of the Ground Ivy, Glechoma
heracea, which used to be called
Alehoof because it was used for
flavouring ale in the Middle Ages
before hops were introduced.
Across the corner of the
field there is a small
rookery; very noisy in
the breeding season.

Rooks in small
numbers are the
farmers' friends as
they take so many grubs
but in larger numbers they
also take large amounts of
the harvest.

Rook

**BEAR RIGHT AND DROP
DOWNHILL SLIGHTLY.**

**TURN LEFT AT THE END
INTO HOOKLEY LANE.**

Ground Ivy

To begin with there is a noticeable contrast between
the gardens here and those at the beginning of the
ramble but further down there is greater similarity and
another fine range of plants. Don't miss the unexpected
architecture of Hookley Close on the left!

TURN LEFT AT THE END to follow the B3001 back to
the starting point. The best building along here is the
Nonconformist Chapel on the left. standing so square
and upright for truth and God.

Willow
Warblers

HANKLEY COMMON : Heathland

DISTANCE: 4 miles approx.

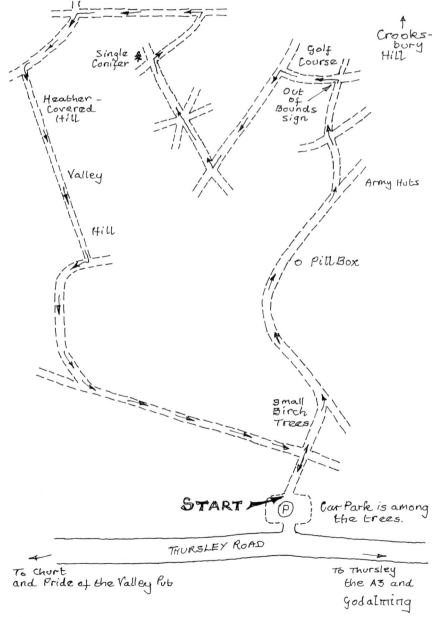

Crooks-
bury
Hill

Golf
Course

Single
Conifer

Out
of
Bounds
sign

Heather –
Covered
Hill

Army Huts

Valley

Hill

o PillBox

small
Birch
Trees

START ➤

ⓟ

Car Park is among
the trees.

THURSLEY ROAD

To Churt
and Pride of the Valley Pub

To Thursley
the A3 and
Godalming

Hankley Common is part of the wilder open country of S.W.Surrey, where it is still possible to find special species of wildlife restricted to such heathland sites, making them of international importance.

Heathland has been lost at such sites as Juniper Valley and Hydon's Ball in this book but, elsewhere, the Surrey Heathland Project is working to save and restore what is left.

PARKING : off the road, between the trees, on the north side of Thursley Road, between Pitch Place and the Pride of the Valley pub. (Grid ref. SU 885392). Thursley is reached from Godalming via Milford and the A3 south, turning right through the central reservation when signed for Thursley.

START walking uphill away from the road, out of the car park, past the military signs. Take the path to the right signed Bridlepath 108.

KEEP STRAIGHT AHEAD to cross the clearing in the trees, keeping the Birch trees on your right.

Wheatea

Such trees are worth checking for bird life, such as
Blue Tits and the less common Long-tailed Tits. They
come not only for the shelter but to search among the
twigs for food. Birch trees support at least 229 species
of insect upon which the birds can feed. In spring and
again in autumn it is worth looking carefully on the
heathland for such passage migrants as the Wheatear,
sketched above.

CONTINUE AHEAD and out into the open.
BEAR LEFT AT THE CROSS TRACKS and keep on the
main track that bears left along the ridge into open
countryside with expansive views out over the valleys
on either side of the crest. Here the heather still
grows, which is the key factor in a true heathland
habitat. Look out for day-flying moths during the summer
months, some of which are particularly colourful and
attractive.

KEEP GOING STRAIGHT ON into the trees. Over on the
right is Crooksbury Hill: the one with the few scraggy
pines on the top – the others were felled during the
First World War. Crooksbury also features in local folk-
lore, if you believe in faeries! Carry on along this
path, passing eventually an old pill box on the right,
left from the Second World War defence system.

CONTINUE until you can see army huts down in the valley and then look for a left fork taking a track off the main bridleway. TAKE THIS LEFT FORK.

CONTINUE downhill, through the conifers and CROSS OVER a main track to continue ahead, through more conifers, until the golf course comes into view.

TURN LEFT by the 'Out of Bounds to Troops' sign, before the golf course.

TURN LEFT AGAIN soon, onto a grass and stone track and upto a cross roads by a demolished brick pillar.

AT THIS JUNCTION TURN RIGHT through the trees on a sand track. Carry on to a meeting of several tracks, like a small roundabout, and STRAIGHT ON up the hill. Look out for Stonechats in the bushes. If they see you coming you may only hear their call note which sounds like two flinty stones being banged together.

STRAIGHT ON AT THE TOP OF THE HILL and stay on this route straight through the next cross tracks, emerging into the open again.

TURN RIGHT

TURN RIGHT at the next cross tracks where there is a solitary conifer on the left. Continue through the heather and birch countryside.

TURN LEFT onto a more open bit of heathland, where Green Woodpeckers often come down to feed on the ants which they pick up with their sticky tongues.

TURN LEFT in this heathland at the next cross tracks and **BEAR LEFT** over the heather-covered hill and down the other side to follow the path uphill again, to **TURN RIGHT** up the next hill again.

Green woodpecker.

TURN LEFT on the top, keeping the trees on your left. This track will take you back to the start.

Looking into the Turn, Pitch Place.

ON THE WAY BACK, PERHAPS, stop at Thursley cricket ground and have a quiet walk up the street to the Saxon church. It retains Saxon windows complete with their wooden frames (a great national rarity) but the whole building is beautiful and full of interest. The design of the timber tower frame is particularly impressive. The street is a narrow lane through cottages and farms and summer flowers; not overdone, quietly satisfying.

Godalming, Surrey
A. Hawkins 1988-5

LINKING THE RAMBLES

The rambles in this book are kept short deliberately, in order to allow time to stop and look and enjoy, but there are obviously people who would prefer to walk much further at a time. They will find that most of the routes in this book can be traced on the Ordnance Survey map or in the Surrey Street Atlas and they will therefore see opportunities to add extra sections to the route.

Within the limitations of this book, the two Unstead rambles and the Farncombe Ramble all pass by the Ram Ciderhouse in Catteshall Lane and so these rambles can be intertwined. For those who wish to stay on surfaced routes the Godalming Town Centre and Farncombe Rambles link together. Either or both link with Eashing. Out in the country, Hydon's Ball and Juniper Valley link by simply crossing the road.

Local Studies: St.Mark's School, Godalming.